What Is Biggest?

A BOOK ABOUT SIZES

BY NICK REBMAN

The Child's World®
childsworld.com

Published by The Child's World®
1980 Lookout Drive • Mankato, MN 56003-1705
800-599-READ • www.childsworld.com

Acknowledgments
The Child's World®: Mary Swensen, Publishing Director
Red Line Editorial: Editorial direction and production
The Design Lab: Design

Photographs ©: iStockphoto, cover (top left), cover (middle right); Ruth Black/Shutterstock Images, cover (top middle), cover (bottom left); Shutterstock Images, cover (top right), cover (bottom middle), 5, 12 (right); Sergey Peterman/iStockphoto, cover (middle left), cover (bottom right); Olesya Feketa/Shutterstock Images, 4 (top); Salim October/Shutterstock Images, 4 (bottom); Val Lawless/Shutterstock Images, 6–7; Paula French/Shutterstock Images, 8–9; Eric Cote/Shutterstock Images, 10 (top); Wavebreakmedia/Shutterstock Images, 10 (bottom); Yaroslav Mishin/Shutterstock Images, 11; Creativa Images/Shutterstock Images, 12 (left); Michael Jung/iStockphoto, 13

ISBN 9781503807662
LCCN 2015958119

Printed in the United States of America
Mankato, MN
June, 2016
PA02306

About the Author

Nick Rebman likes to write, draw, and travel. He lives in Minnesota.

Some things are big.
Some things are small.
Can you answer these
questions about sizes?

Three friends eat fruit outside. Martina has a watermelon. Shawna has an apple. Molly has some grapes.

Which fruit is biggest?

Jin has many pillows on his bed. Some pillows are brown. Two pillows are yellow. One pillow is orange.

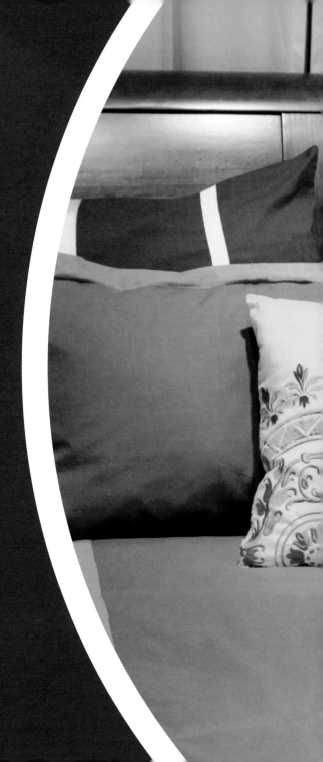

Which pillow is smallest?

We are looking at wild animals. We see some zebras. We see a giraffe. We see elephants too.

Which
animal is
tallest?

Three students are getting books from the library. Sam has brown hair. Brad has black hair. Anna has blond hair.

Whose hair is shortest?

Three boys are dressed up for a nice dinner. Dan is wearing a blue tie with stripes. Ethan is wearing a black tie. Caleb is wearing a red tie with stripes.

Whose tie is widest?

ANSWER KEY

The watermelon
is biggest.

The orange pillow
is smallest.

The giraffe is tallest.

Brad's hair is shortest.

Dan's tie is widest.

GLOSSARY

biggest (BIG-ist) The biggest thing is larger than everything else. Martina had the biggest fruit.

shortest (SHORT-ist) The shortest thing is lower than everything else. Brad's hair was shortest.

smallest (SMALL-ist) The smallest thing is littler than everything else. The orange pillow was smallest.

tallest (TALL-ist) The tallest thing is higher than everything else. The giraffe was tallest.

widest (WYD-ist) The widest thing is larger from side to side than everything else. Dan's tie was widest.

TO LEARN MORE

IN THE LIBRARY

Greenwood, Marie. *Real-Size Baby Animals*. New York: DK Publishing, 2012.

Hall, Katharine. *Polar Bears and Penguins*. Mount Pleasant, SC: Sylvan Dell Publishing, 2014.

Pistoia, Sara. *Shapes*. Mankato, MN: Child's World, 2014.

ON THE WEB

Visit our Web site for links about sizes: childsworld.com/links

Note to Parents, Teachers, and Librarians: We routinely verify our Web links to make sure they are safe and active sites. So encourage your readers to check them out!

INDEX

animals, 8–9

giraffes, 8

pillows, 6–7

elephants, 8

hair, 10–11

ties, 12–13

fruit, 4–5

zebras, 8